THE DAUGHTER WE DIDN'T KNOW WE HAD

The Tears, Fears, and Joys of a Mother of a Transgender Child

Marilyn Phillips

authorHOUSE®

AuthorHouse™ LLC
1663 Liberty Drive
Bloomington, IN 47403
www.authorhouse.com
Phone: 1-800-839-8640

Published by AuthorHouse   09/05/2014

ISBN: 978-1-4969-3740-7 (sc)
ISBN: 978-1-4969-3739-1 (e)

Library of Congress Control Number: 2014915590

Any people depicted in stock imagery provided by Thinkstock are models,
and such images are being used for illustrative purposes only.
Certain stock imagery © Thinkstock.

Dedicated to

My husband without whom I would not have the courage to write this book.

My youngest son who was there at the start and kept the humor going.

My beautiful daughter who's strength is a source of pride for us.

And finally for

My wonderful Sammy who may be gone from our lives but will live forever in our hearts.

CONTENTS

INTRODUCTION

By

Rachel and Marilyn

I am a Girl

This is my contribution to my mother's book, the one you are reading now (I guess that goes without saying though).

I am a girl. That should be all I have to say about this subject, but sadly this is not the case. Sadly we live in a world where I am stuck with my former identity plaguing my life. Even this book is a reminder of that fact, and it bugs me.

However I have decided to make a contribution to this project to try and help bring this world to a place where I can just say "I am a girl" and not have anyone question me about it.

I was of course born with male parts between my legs. The way I explain it is; I was born with a genetic deformity that caused me to be born with male parts instead of female parts, but I was always a girl.

This explaination is difficult for most people to understand. Although I was "born a boy" and raised as such, I have never identified as a boy. I always knew that I was a girl, but by some fluke of divine stupidity, or biological incompetence, I was born with the wrong parts. This resulted in me being raised as a boy, and taught to reach for male expectations.

My earliest memory was from when I was four, asking my mother to buy me a "Sailor Moon" costume. I remember every wish that I ever made, be it wishing wells or birthday candles, was always to be seen as the girl I really was.

Puberty was a nightmare for me. I feared becoming manly. I feared having facial hair. Thankfully I turned out to be a very fem looking "boy", but people still saw me as a boy, as him, the imposter. Talking about my past is all well and good, but what I really need to talk about are my feelings towards my past, and my former self.

I hate him, the "former" me, the imposter, the mask, the life stealer. I hate the fact that there will always be part of him plaguing my life in some fashion. Everything I accomplished, was credited to him and not me. Everyone loved him, but not me, they didn't know me. Every fiber of my being wants to erase him from memory, time, and knowledge. All I want more than anything is to just be another everyday girl.

I am lucky enough that I don't look obvious enough for anyone to clue into my former identity, but every so often someone will ask me. It is the worst feeling in the world when someone asks me "did you used to be a boy?" Because I want to just answer "no" because as far as I am concerned, I never was. I gave that answer to someone once, and they called me a liar. I am not lying when I say "I was never a boy." Just because I had the parts, does not mean I was anything other than a girl. Just because I was raised as such, does not mean I wasn't a girl. I have always been a girl.

Which brings me to my next point. I hate being called transgendered, transsexual, transgirl, or anything else with a trans label on it. Why do I have to differentiate myself from any other girl? The answer is that I shouldn't have to. I am not transgendered. I am not trans-anything. I am just a girl: who happened to be born with a genetic deformity that resulted in me having the wrong parts at birth. But I am still just a girl.

Of course, inevitably, when I get close enough with someone I will eventually have to tell them. And almost always they say, "I kinda knew a little bit." as if that would give me comfort. It doesn't. To hear someone tell me that they kinda already know about how I "used to be a boy" just makes all my insecurities about my femininity blow out of preportion. It makes me feel like that my struggle to show the world who I really am was all for not.

I know that my past is not obvious; by the simple fact that men hit on me on a daily basis. Which at first was awesome, because it re-assured my femininity, but is kind of getting old now... but still kinda nice.

I apologize for this being written as a rant, but this is how my mind normally works. Now back to the topic at hand.

I guess I will finish my little contribution with my feelings about this book. When mom first told me that she was going to write this book, I hated the idea and I still do. Writing these words down for publication is actually very difficult for me, even though it is anonymous.

This book is being writing to try and help families with individuals such as myself, and I understand this. But at the same time this book brings out the possibility of my greatest fear coming true, the fear that I will never be rid of him, the imposter.

Even though I know that being completely rid of him is not realistic, it is still the thing that I desire most, and I feel like that this book is counter acting that goal. But it is a sacrifice, however begrudgungly, I am making to try and help others like me and their families with this issue. So please don't let this be in vain.

I know this was hard for Rachel to write but I hope she will one day come to realize that it is because I am so proud of her that I want the world to know that my little girl deserves to be happy.

But I don't think she will every be fully happy until she reaches the point where she can reitergate Sammy into her life so that they again can be one.

I feel that she needs someone to blame; somewhere to direct her anger. For her family there is no separating the two; they are one. It was the strength of her other self that allowed her to do what she felt was right.

She is still the same person who accomplished all those great things; we have all heard the phrase spoken by Juliet in "Romeo and Juliet":

".......what's in a name? that which we call a rose by any other name would smell as sweet......"

Had Rachel not been so eager to toss Sammy aside; I truly believe her transformation would have been easier on her and her family as well.

She has spoken to us of not wanting to be labeled by being called transgender; she feels it will impede her leaving her past behind and move on. She is right in so far as that it allows others to point and label her as some sort of demon.

The term transgender is but another name and helps others identify something they may otherwise not be able to discuss. If you do not allow it to define you then it is no more different then being called a diabetic. A condition which needs to be addressed and taken care off.

I understand that until we are able to convince the rest of the world of that fact we will have to deal with the label. I didn't allow the professionals back in her school days to place labels on her which will follow her all her life and cause harm and I won't allow it now.

My child was born with a defect which did not match her inner self; she is not a freak of nature or a victim of lack of nurturing.

She is a gift from the Gods and I am thankful for her. I will miss that special person who came to me so many years ago and I hope one day to have a reunion with that person.

But for now I will have to put the needs of my child ahead of my own.

I hope this book will help everyone better understand the ups and downs of a family in transition and find the strength to stand together.

Marilyn Phillips

Adversity is a fact of life. It can't be controlled. What we can control is how we react to it.

You are my rose, so full of thorns

All I ever do is look after you

I prick my finger and I get angry

But as I look down at

you in your crib

All I can smell is the

sweetness of my rose.

CHAPTER ONE

How do you react when your son tells you he is in transition to become a woman?

My reaction was to crack a joke. I had just driven for two hours from my home in a small rural town to the city to pick him up and bring him down for a visit.

Having my handsome, wonderful son, Sammy, say to me that he wanted to be a girl was a statement which sent a chill through me, how do you respond to such a thing?

At the time we were driving on the highway traveling at 110km/hour (68/miles/hr.), and the only thing which came out of my mouth was, "That's a great thing to tell me when we are traveling at 110 km/hr down the highway."

We both laughed at the obscurity of the moment, we had often shared a laugh but this time it was different. I tried hard to hide my disappointment from him, but I knew he felt it.

How could he not? From that moment on both our lives, and the lives of the rest of our family, would be changed forever. In ways hard to image, and too sad to want to even consider, but now you have to, there it is in front of you.

You have nowhere to go, unless you crash that huge hunk of steel into the nearest light standard, you have to support your child or you walk away.

You sit there unable to escape, listening while he tells you how this all came to be, listening while you think to yourself how will his father take this, does his brother know?

How are you to explain it to others? For twenty years you've told everyone you have two sons, how do you suddenly explain having a daughter? Perhaps from a previous marriage, perhaps an infant put up for adoption has found you.

Yes, those are all possible answers. But where has your son gone, let's explain that one. Moved overseas, kind of young for that, maybe died, yes, but what about funeral arrangements?

You could say, "He was cremated, no service".

It is amazing what your mind will throw out at you when you're in a state of shock even while driving down the highway at death defying speeds and you think, "There is something I should be doing right now, what is it"?

Driving!

Is this the end of the tale? No it isn't even the beginning!

The beginning is some twenty years earlier when my wonderful child came into the world. The day when I told myself I would do everything in my power to protect this tiny bundle from all the hardships the world would throw at him.

Like every new parent we were confident in our abilities to do just that; we were parents of the modern age and were well aware of all the complications that could arise in our little champ's life.

He was born healthy and he would live happy; we would accept and love him no matter what. In the beginning we couldn't have imagined anything that would challenge our love for our child.

 We were wrong---the years ahead would challenge our patience, our ideas on parenting, our sanity and our views of ourselves as accepting, loving parents.

Sammy's announcement was the beginning of a hard road that would bring things back from the past.

I wasn't totally surprised by his announcement; I knew something wasn't right with my son for some time.

It seemed from the moment he was born; his life was to be a struggle. They say a mother knows things, can feel things about their child that others can't detect.

From the moment he was born I had a feeling deep inside of me that seemed to warn me of things to come but as a new mother I didn't see it as anything more than nerves.

Sometimes the fear of what I felt made me push the feelings to the back of my mind. As the years passed and the feelings grew stronger I started to pay more attention to them; I could no longer deny them.

At the moment when Sammy told me that he was in transition; I suddenly realized that all those fears and feelings were pointing to this.

There were many signs over the years that something was coming. Things I thought were minor incident at the time suddenly made sense. And suddenly I saw them as the stepping stones to where I now found myself.

Life to this point wasn't easy for Sammy on so many levels; he had endured many hurdles that any parent would kill to prevent. The struggles and the tears of the last twenty years had torn a huge hole in my heart as I failed to protect him. And now this!

If he had said he was gay I would not have been surprised; since he was a young child our friends kept hinting to us that he was gay. To be honest it had crossed my mind a time or two; but I really didn't care if he was as I had several friends when I was younger who were gay – I loved them.

I would have been concerned for him as I saw first-hand the discrimination my friends suffered and I wasn't looking forward to my child having to endure that.

When Sammy was younger he loved the color pink, the show "Sailor Moon" was one of his favorites.

In his teenage years he loved to wear costumes depicting characters from his books; but since it was something that all his friends were doing as well I pushed it to the back of my mind as nothing to worry about.

Even though he often preferred to dress as the female characters and wear wigs; of which he had several, I tried to think of it as nothing to worry about.

However those feelings of something being wrong were never far from my mind.

I was right and this sudden announcement from Sammy although I was temporarily shocked and I tried to laugh it off; I knew we all were in for a rough ride.

This wasn't going to be easy on anyone especially Sammy and I feared for how he would be treated. I feared someone would hurt him in ways I didn't want my mind to consider.

He was my baby and he and I had developed a wonderful relationship over the years. I didn't want to suddenly become the parent who wasn't supportive.

Yet, I couldn't stop thinking about how this was going to affect me; that is terrible I know but my fight or flight instinct kicked in. No one would want to face this if they had a choice and I am no different.

A strong part of me wanted to protect my child and still another part of me wanted to protect myself.

I knew that the worst was to come and there was only one thing to do; and that was to not let my child down.

My book is about the upheaval and emotional turmoil that started on that day and continues to this; each day is still a struggle for my child and for us as a family.

I want to show how that day took us on an extraordinary journey that tested our patience and our love for our child.

The struggle each day to keep on track and be able to give to my child what he needed while still being able to get what our family needed. The two are not always the same, but the one whose needs are the most desperate seem to win out.

How do you come to terms with the loss of a child and the sudden introduction of someone who you do not know but you are expected to love and support?

The book tells how as a family we each tried to make the best out of this new situation; to come to terms with it and try to stay a family. Starting that day we struggle to make it through this trying time; and there were times when I thought we would fail.

It was a journey that took us from struggling with; to understanding the meaning of "Gender Identity", while trying to sort out all the emotions that suddenly invaded our minds.

We had to come to terms with feelings of anger and confusion and try to replace them with ones of pride and acceptance. There were meetings with counselors, physicians, psychiatrists and discussions of the surgery which would transform our son into our daughter.

Each and every day I am burdened with the question of— Did I cause this? I go from feeling that I have done a great job with my kids to feeling like the worst parent in the world. There are days I feel anger at my child for dropping this on me, I feel like I did all the right things and yet this happens.

My perception of "Nature vs Nurture" was turned upside down, what I thought was once the way is no more. My feelings of charity come into question as I wonder why I should be charitable if the Gods dare to do this to me.

I am writing this book not just to help myself come to terms with what has taken place but also to let others in this situation understand that there is a happy end if you let go of the multitude of emotions which block your way to acceptance while realizing that your feelings are important.

Take the time to be angry, take the time to enjoy the new, and above all let go of the guilt you will feel. That is what I believe, that is what I have to believe, what else can you believe?

It isn't easy and there are days I wish I didn't have to get out of bed but there are also days of pride that we made it this far.

Each day I will miss the little boy who grew to a young man that I never got to say goodbye to.

My husband best sums up this new adventure for us.

While Sammy was going through the process of transformation from male to female my husband spoke with one of his doctors and this is how John described her: "She is the daughter I didn't know I had."

It didn't mean sudden acceptance but it was the start for my husband to openly facing his fears and doubts which I hope will put him on the road to recovery.

Our other child, Blaine also had to come to terms with this new person in his life. A person he called brother was now someone he had to introduce as his sister.

His confusion manifested itself in the form of anger; and he found comfort inside a bottle. He was only nineteen at the time and was struggling with issues of his own.

But together we are managing to keep the wheels turning and if one wheel falls off or becomes loose the others help put it back on. That is what families do – help and support is the backbone of family life.

We aren't the best at it, there were times when someone had to chase the wheel down the road and retrieve it; (this is just a part of my silly humor, my kids tell me that I am crazy but they love me anyway).

Having your child tell you that they want to change their gender will be a statement which will send you into all types of emotional upheaval.

I want this book to tell the truth about what happened along the way; where we went wrong, where we succeeded and what brought us to where we are now. What events took us to this point and examine whether we could have done something different.

I hope doing so will allow others going through this with their loved one to discover that all is not lost. To give you hope and for you to realize that you are not losing someone dear to you but you are being introduced to a new version of that loved one.

We gained a child who is happy and confident in herself; someone who isn't afraid to stand up for herself and who has more strength and courage then anyone I know.

It won't be easy; there will be hard days and plenty of them. There will be plenty of tears and maybe even a few harsh words but there should always remain plenty of love.

There are days when I cry for no apparent reason; I lie in bed at night and I begin to laugh and cry at the same time when I think of something our son did that amused me. I laugh at his funny side and I cry because I feel that I will never again be able to see that wonderful smile.

I can't let go of that face; that smile. If I do I will lose a part of myself; and someone special that I loved and cared for all those years.

I still see the wonderful boy who loved trains, who the nurse laid across my chest the day he was born. The boy who crawled into my lap and listened while his father read him a story, who looked so happy and was ready to conquer the world.

The boy who grew into a young man and who made us proud as he faced down the challenges that he met each and every day of his life; the young man who loved science and wanted to live to be 200 and see the human race reach out to the stars.

These are my memories which I will struggle to hold on to.

There will be new memories made with this new person who has suddenly made herself a part of our family.

A new person who will leave our son behind and follow a path of her own choosing; one we will try to make easier for her.

Chapter Two

Our son, Sammy, "Samuel Patrick" was born in October; he was our little pumpkin having been born so close to Halloween. He was the perfect package of health, weighting in at a little over 7 lbs. and 23 inches.

The doctor asked how he got to be so long since both of his parents were lucky to be barely over 5 foot tall, my husband was 5ft 4 ins. and I was barely coming in at 5ft 2 ins.

We proudly took him home and started on our path to being the perfect parents, determined to do all the right things for our new born; the perfect model, of the perfect parents, and the perfect family.

From that moment on we would not allow anything to get in the way of his happiness.

John worked on the road in those early days: he came home late Fridays and left again late Sunday. I was left alone with a new baby and I would hate when Sundays came.

I cried from the time I got up on Sunday until he left; I was angry at us both; John for leaving me and at myself; I always vowed to never rely on someone else for happiness...

Our departures were tearful and full of anguish; I would sulk throughout the week, do a mad clean on Thursday and be full of cheer when he returned Friday.

Looking back it would not surprise me to know I suffered post-partum depression. Or maybe I was just feeling sorry for myself either way only a few short months later, John quit that job and moved on to something which kept him home during the week.

And the end result was the arrival of our beautiful new boy Blaine; just 53 weeks after the birth of Sammy. We didn't mind we were happy again, and the future looked bright. We were going to be the model for the perfect modern family.

We seemed to be starting off right.

Blaine was a quiet child, unlike his brother who was colic for 8 months, from the start Blaine slept through the night. The boys quickly formed a bond as they grew from infants into lively toddlers.

When we took them out they were quite often mistaken for twins.

We soon developed a few family traditions that others might find odd; such as taking a picnic basket full of goodies out to the park in the dead of winter.

It was so peaceful and quiet, the kids were the focus of our full attention and they loved it. We took them skiing in the Rockies each Easter and I loved seeing the faces of my babies as they chatted endlessly about the day they spent on the slopes with their father.

Before too long it was time for Sammy to start kindergarten; we gleamed proudly as he stood at the door with his book bag. This was the start of a bright and beautiful future for our child; from here on nothing would stand in the way of him conquering the world.

Sammy seemed like a happy boy, he made friends quickly; he was liked by his teachers and always had a playdate.

I was the mother I said I was going to be, I always invited his friends in the house, and I signed up for teacher's helper at his school. I helped with pizza days; became a member of the school board and when he wanted to join Scouts both his father and I became leaders.

There wasn't anything we weren't going to do to make both of our kids happy. The following year when Blaine started kindergarten he fell right in behind his brother and they seemed to be conquering all that came their way.

One summer Sammy seemed to be suffering from a cold that seemed to take too long to go away. Doctors seemed to think he was just a slow healer and told me to stop being a worrying mother. I suffered from allergies from the time I was in my mid-teens and I knew the symptoms; I knew he needed help.

And soon I found a doctor willing to listen; after seeing an allergist Sammy was diagnosed with Asthma and he was said to have only about 10% lung capacity. He was giving a special machine to help him breath. But he still often ended up in emergency.

As a result of his condition he developed a few habits which were beyond his control. One of which was sniffing and rubbing his nose; in no time this became a source of teasing among many of his classmates.

At about the same time he started to show signs of behavior problems which baffled the school and his doctor. He was now in grade 1 and his teacher called me each day to say Sammy's behavior was getting worse.

On one occasion the teacher found him under his desk and he seemed to not know why; he couldn't sit still and fumbled about with his pencils and books. He didn't seem to be able to hold his attention on one task at a time and was quickly falling behind his classmates.

At home it was impossible to get him to sit at the table long enough to do homework. If I didn't sit beside him and constantly probe him to keep going, he would start to fidget. He seemed lost when he looked away from his books and couldn't tell which problem he was on.

His reading skills were well below that of his classmates; yet he seemed to be intelligent.

He could tell you things that astonished you and he loved museums; we would go every chance we got. He loved anything to do with outer space, geology, science, chemistry and he loved to draw.

He has a natural talent for drawing and began to create things he saw on TV or in movies; he seemed to be a natural engineer. Yet his attention span was limited when he was in a controlled environment; to the point where he couldn't get anything done.

His sleep became interrupted and he most often didn't fall asleep until 3 or 4 in the morning. Getting him up for school was a daily chore I didn't enjoy.

He knew he was having problems even at that young an age; but he never complained or made excuses. His frustration often mounted to tears and head pounding; it was enough to break my heart.

The so called experts didn't seem to know what was wrong and even worse it took months to get to see one. We were shuffled from one expert to another with months of waiting in between.

All the while the bullying at school mounted as teasing about his allergies escalated to his being called stupid because of his as yet still unknown challenges

His temper soon became a problem and he began to lash out. Often he would come home in tears because he was bullied and called vicious names.

School, which he once loved, became a place of horror and it tore my heart out each day as I sent him of to what I knew would be hell.

The teachers seemed helpless to do anything about the bullying or didn't care enough to do something about it.

From elementary school to high school the bullying would follow him and the escalation became apparent to everyone.

When the kids were young I worked from home running my own business. This allowed me to be around for my children and not having to farm them out to a day care center. This allowed me to develop a tremendously close relationship with both of my sons.

John and I made sure each boy got their own time with us. John would take them, one at a time, to sporting events like hockey.

I would pick them up from school for a "date" where we would sit and talk about anything that they wanted to discuss.

No topic was off limits and we had great times together. We both wanted to make sure that neither of our boys would feel that they couldn't come to us with any problem or concern.

Sammy loved his dates with me; we kept doing them even when he was in high school. Blaine soon felt that he was too old and was more comfortable going with dad to the games.

The bond that formed between Sammy and I was one that I never thought would be broken by anything.

Those tortured days when he came home after enduring the daily bullying when we would talk, the walks we would take, the times I drove him to his after school activities cemented our bond.

---m---

His brother Blaine had been born with a hernia which didn't become apparent until about age 4.

We enrolled both boys in skating and swimming at early ages and while Sammy took to both easily; Blaine struggled and didn't seem interested.

When he attended pre-school at our local YMCA the staff commented on how he didn't want to do any activities and was a slow walker.

We had noticed that even though he started walking at 10 months he preferred to scoot along the floor.

We were already dealing with Sammy's problems with asthma and his problems with attention at school. We weren't sure what we would be in for with Blaine.

Our perfect children suddenly were testing our resolve; could we still be the perfect parents we wanted to be inspite of these seemingly endless problems?

When Blaine's hernia was finally diagnosed and treated we instantly noticed a change in his activity level.

You couldn't hold him down anymore; it was as if he wanted to make up for 4 years of missing out.

He became a whole new person and his true charm came bubbling out. Within a short time his comic nature came shining through, and it became obvious where his interests lay.

His doctor told us that he had been living in pain all that time; was it any wonder he was in no mood to do activities?

"There," we thought, "one problem solved. Now if only we would get Sammy on the right path."

The next year Blaine started kindergarten and Sammy seemed pleased to have his little brother tag along. Because they had the same friends it was easy to organize play dates and birthday parties.

Then again a problem popped up; Blaine began to show the same signs of inattention as Sammy had the previous year.

Now I had two boys who couldn't sit still and with whom I had to struggle daily to get homework completed.

John and I were at a loss to know what was happening with our sons. At home we had no problems getting them interested in things. They would sit and listen to John reading to them, and they would play games.

When John took them to sporting events they would sit for hours and watch what was happening. What was going on at school that made them act so different?

I thought that if I volunteered at school I would be able to see what might be going on; but there didn't seem to be a straight forward answer.

We took them both to have their eyes checked, Sammy often rubbed his eyes. The doctor put it down to allergies and Blaine didn't seem to have any eye problems.

Then the doctor said they both had ADHD-Attention Deficit Hyperactivity Disorder- and they were both put on meds. It didn't take more than a month when both boys stated they didn't want to take the meds anymore.

We explained to them that the meds were to help with the ADHD; and if they wanted to stop we would have to find other ways to control the ADHD.

They agreed and they worked hard and managed to succeed at recognizing when they were getting out of hand.

Blaine soon settled down and was doing quite nicely in school. We were pleased that he had done so well and soon our attention was back on Sammy.

There seemed to be more going on than the ADHD; he couldn't still concentrate and he seemed disorganized. His reading was slow, his writing unreadable and he was never able to finish an assignment.

He was barely making it from grade to grade. As the work got harder the problems he was having seemed to become more obvious.

On parent/teacher nights his teachers would all tell us how bright he was and how they knew he could do the work. Yet they couldn't tell us why or what the problem may be.

We had been waiting for two years for him to be declared bad enough to be referred to professionals.

Finally in grade three he was sent to see professionals in psychology, physical therapy and early childhood education.

The conclusion was that Sammy suffered from dyslexia, ADHD, OCD (Obsessive Compulsive Disorder) motor tics and mild fine motor delay; at least now we had some answers but still we had to find solutions to help him.

His OCD seemed to be causing the greatest problem; his father and I noticed that it was interfering with his daily activities and wondered if it was having the same effects on his school work.

At home he would have to do tasks in a particular order and if he couldn't he would get very upset. When getting dressed, for example, if he couldn't find a sock he wanted he wouldn't use another pair because those socks went with the clothes he was wearing. He wouldn't put on his right glove before his left glove; both of his socks had to be at the same height.

This last item caused us great anxiety because quite often when we were crossing at an intersection he would have to stop and pull up his socks.

I mentioned this to his teacher and she immediately knew what I was speaking about. She said that he would not start a task if he was not able to find his supplies in the right order; for example, he would have to take things out of his desk in a specific order – his pen, his eraser, his writing pad, and if he couldn't find his eraser he couldn't take his pad out because it was not in the right order.

He wasn't able to finish a test because if he got stuck on question two he couldn't go on to question three because it would cause things to be out of order.

If we tried to get him to do things out of his preferred order then he would get upset. I did not know what he felt would happen if he mixed things up and he couldn't explain it either; it just gave him a feeling that something bad would happen.

Finally with a lot of encouragement he began to try doing things out of order and when he realized the world would not suddenly stop he began to make remarkable improvement.

I told him to try doing his test questions out of order and if he didn't know an answer to go on to the next question and if he had time come back to it.

He gave it a try one day and was very excited when he came home and much to his delight he finally got his first A.

Unfortunately for Sammy the school house bullying would soon be taken to the extreme and an issue we had to deal with throughout his school years. His suffering would make my heart ache daily and often left me in tears as I struggled to find answers. The long years ahead didn't seem to be ever going to come to an end.

Thankfully my son is a strong person and his wonderful spirit and maturity was his best defense. His determination to not let them win or drag him down helped him succeed in his one love – Air Cadets. There he thrived and showed his many talents which allowed him to prove to himself his true worth.

But the true test of his strength and spirit was to come later.

My son was often called a homosexual, to girly, a sissy and other hurtful words. He was a small child both in height and weight. He wasn't into sports, loved music and drawing and felt more at ease with adults than children his own age.

He was polite, kind and a young gentleman; at our church he was called "our little minister" by the congregation.

He was a bright child in spite of having Attention Deficit Disorder and Obsessive Compulsive Disorder, he learned by watching rather than reading.

We encouraged his interest and never doubted his ability to do anything he wanted. But there were days when we weren't sure if the taunting and bullying would end and if our little soldier would make it through.

By the time he was set to graduate from high school and had had much success at his beloved Air Cadets we felt he was on his way to succeeding.

I knew his tormentors were wrong about him; he wasn't the weakling they tagged him as and I was sure he would prove me right.

Now that he was away from them and doing what he wanted I felt more relaxed – the feeling didn't last long.

At age 18 he revealed to me his thoughts of suicide which didn't really shock me as I often worried about it; he had suffered so and I knew that teenage suicide was often related to being bullied.

Our family knew first-hand about teenage suicide; my niece killed herself just three days from her eighteenth birthday. She was just six years older than Sammy.

I had often asked him if he was suicidal but he had reassured me that he wasn't but honestly who could endure that much misery without feeling low?

This revelation bothered me because he would say he was going to live forever, and live to see many wonderful inventions especially in space.

But still the thought that my child considered suicide saddened and frightened me, and we were determined to get him help. Soon he was seeing a counselor and doing well as far as his father and I could see.

Counselling wasn't the end of it merely the start; things were happening fast and we were concerned.

Counselling began him thinking of different things like homosexuality and transgender issues. His father was upset with the message the counselor seemed to be suggesting. He was being vague about what he thought Sammy's problem was; he wanted Sammy to tell us himself. John was not about to accept this and told both Sammy and the counselor so.

Sammy continued to see the counselor for several more sessions but instead of it giving him answers it seemed to introduce more questions.

Our reaction to his sessions made him keep things bottled up inside and he never spoke of the matter to us again until that day in 2010.

I tried to keep talking to him about things but he seemed to have come to the conclusion that we would not understand and would stand in his way.

No matter what I said he just seemed to not want to come to us anymore. I could see he was suffering and I feared the worst was about to happen.

I feared he would commit suicide or run away; each day his struggle burned a hole in my heart. I didn't know what to do; I felt stuck between my husband and my son. I knew how John felt so how could I convince him that Sammy needed him to listen without judging.

I knew Sammy was in need of help and I had no way to help him; I had no quick answers. As the days, weeks and months passed and the talking fell off I hoped a solution would miraculously manifest itself out of thin air.

I hoped one day I would be able to help everyone be happy. I hoped each day that at the end we would still be a family.

Denial does no one any good it only prolongs the inevitable; why had we not had the strength then and there to say "yes" to our child. To give him all he needed and tell him we will stand behind his decisions.

Whatever they may be?

Our responsibility was to ensure his decisions didn't harm him. Our blindness to the truth not only caused our child to suffer longer than necessary – it cost us the opportunity to say goodbye to the son we loved and accept this new person who was soon to be part of our family.

CHAPTER THREE

―――――――――――∞―――――――――――

In 2010 John and I moved to a small town; John's job had been relocated but the boys decided that they wanted to stay behind and find their own apartment.

They both wanted to attend local colleges and didn't want to leave their friends; so we found them an apartment close to where they worked and with easy access to school.

It was hard for them to be without us at first but they seemed to quickly settle in. Both boys were working at local, yet different movie theaters. They were both trying to make ends meet and we helped out when we could.

We were settling in our new home and I had opened a small store. John was enjoying his new job and even though I never thought I would like living in a small town; the place quickly grew on me.

John and I knew the boys were having struggles living on minimum wage and we encouraged them to work towards the future they wanted.

Our kids from an early age knew what they wanted to be.

Blaine wanted to be a comedian, actor and movie director. We never once said that those goals were too lofty to achieve. Why couldn't he be all those things?

At the age of 12, we introduced him to the manager of a local comedy club. After talking to us for about an hour he said he would allow Blaine to come to open mic night.

Blaine was thrilled and I called to book a time for an upcoming Wednesday open mic night. I wasn't going to waste this opportunity so I contacted our local paper to explain what was happening.

They agreed to send out a reporter the night Blaine was to perform. It turned out that that very night they were doing a live radio show and some of the top comedians in the country were to perform.

This little bit of news didn't shake our Blaine; heavens no he was too busy taking it all in. Not only was the place packed but the owner of the comedy club was in attendance.

Blaine was number 24 out of 25 performers that night. After it was over we were ready to burst with pride; the club owner came to us after and stated that, "That boy has talent and he can perform here anytime."

The paper article was most complimentary and we proudly framed it. The next open mic night Blaine was there in full form.

After that first night I couldn't attend anymore, my poor nerves couldn't take it. I went to a few others but I never got used to people judging my baby.

Blaine continued to perform for several years and he added acting to his resume. Doing several school plays such as, "The Importance of Being Ernest", and "The Music Man".

For the last two school years he worked on the school's radio and did videos for the school. After school he decided he wanted to turn his attention to becoming a director. His love of movies is very evident in his large collection of DVDs.

He also has a blog he does on movies and I am pleased to say he calls me regularly to talk about his latest project and the latest movie he has seen.

Although growing up the boys were not extremely close; they did have a great sibling relationship. Since their interests were so different there was no rivalry.

Sammy fell in love with air cadets and joined as soon as he could. Sammy was always great at drawing and design; he loved planes and as soon as he could he wanted to join cadets to learn to be a pilot. He loved being a mentor to the younger cadets and was part of the drill team, an instructor and played in the band.

He seemed destined to fulfill his dreams and as far as we knew was very happy. He looked like a young man fully aware of where life would take him.

When we moved away and they shared an apartment they had the usual arguments about whose turn it was to clean the bathroom. But until Sammy decided he was transgender they were good friends.

As they grew older their friends changed and since they no longer shared the same friends; they didn't socialize together much.

Blaine was there to witness first- hand the problems associated with Sammy being transgender. He knew about his brother long before we did.

He never mentioned it to us; later he told me he felt it wasn't his place to do so. He felt that Sammy would tell us when he was ready.

Shortly after we had moved to our new home, Sammy started to see a psychologist about his problems and after work would dress as a female.

This was a part of his therapy to see if it made him feel more like the person he felt he should be. At the same time he started taking medication to stop his male hormone production and estrogen to help replace male testosterone with female hormones.

Blaine soon recognized an extreme shift in his brother's mood. He became angry and at times violent; often having outbursts of tears and rage.

Sammy also decided at that time that he no longer wanted to go by his given name and Blaine as well as his friends began to call him by his chosen female name, "Rachel".

Blaine told me he was shocked by her announcement she was female; if she had said she was gay then he would have understood.

It is unfortunate that Blaine doesn't seem to have a lot of memories of his time with his brother. Those memories seem to have been blurred by Blaine's own feelings of neglect.

He had to struggle with the attention his brother was getting; first as a result of Sammy's learning difficulties which took a lot of our time. And by the fact that Sammy participated in a lot of activities which required one or both of us to be a part of such as air cadets.

Blaine doesn't seem to remember that they were both scouts together or that we introduced him to the comedy Club and signed him up for acting lessons.

There were many times when we tried to get Blaine involved in activities once his hernia had been fixed but he rarely seemed interested in organized activity.

Each morning I would drive Sammy to school; mainly because it took him so long to get organized in the morning if I didn't drive him he would be late.

I would ask Blaine if he wanted to drive with us but he always refused saying he was off to meet friends and didn't want to be late; even if he was leaving the same time as we were.

He would jump on his bike and be gone; even when he didn't use his bike he would prefer to walk.

I didn't understand it then but I do now Blaine has admitted he felt neglected when growing up; it seemed to him that we were always too busy with Sammy. He also decided to see a psychologist about his feelings and he seems to have come to terms with the past.

As boys together they had many great times but by Blaine's own admission he sees his brother and now his sister as more of a background character in his life.

I know his biggest concern when his brother announced his transition was that he would live to regret it. That he/she would one day wake up and think: what have I done?

I don't think there will be any chance of that happening.

Blaine has had to deal with friends asking what has happened to his brother. The reaction would often be from slight surprise to a general feeling of shock.

Some asked polite questions while others avoided the topic. Eventually the questions stopped as the word got around.

As with us; Blaine tends to not bring up the subject with new people that he meets. How do you bring up such a subject?

This is a quote from Blaine:

"I think Sammy lived a short, tortured life by either his own hand or the hand of others, and disappeared without realizing how loved he was regardless."

Inspite of what my baby Blaine says to me that statement says he loved and misses his brother.

John and I have tried to make things up to Blaine by supporting him in his ambitions to become a Director. Whether we need to make things up to him or whether it is merely our perception we can't let him down now.

He has grown into a very strong, independent and courageous young man of whom we are very proud.

He has finally come to realize that his father and I didn't abandon him in favor of his brother. We have no doubt that he is capable of standing on his own two feet.

And we are hopeful that someday he will forgive Sammy and will be proud to show his children off to their Aunt Rachel.

While Blaine had doubts about Sammy's behavior, he never gave away his secret.

. . . .

The way in which Rachel told me about her transition (driving down the road at 110km) was inconvenient but the way in which I told her father wasn't any better.

I had known about it for about two months at that time; John had been away for quite a while and had only recently returned home.

I told both kids that I wanted to tell their father; I knew he wasn't going to take it well and I was not sure what he would actually do about it.

On occasion John's work required that he visit the head office which was in the same city as where the kids lived. He always made sure he took the time to take them out to dinner and make a grocery run with them.

On this one occasion I knew he would see Rachel in full female form. All day I tried to come up with some way to tell him; which words to use?

I was at a loss for any but I couldn't let him just walk in to the apartment and see his child as a female and not know what was going on.

I was standing in the kitchen while he prepared to go; he always stayed overnight with friends of ours and he was still packing his bag.

Until the moment he walked into the kitchen I had no idea how to tell him; and I couldn't believe the words that popped out of my mouth when he walked through the door.

"Sammy says he wants to be a girl. And he has been living as a girl for some time now."

The shattered look that crossed his face that day still haunts me; he understood exactly what I said. I was thankful for that because I wasn't sure I would be able to repeat it.

While he stood there in silence I tried to explain how I was informed and why I didn't tell him before. I am not sure what words I used they were all pouring out of me in rapid succession.

If I stopped I might not get started again and I knew he had to know. I feared at first he might hit me, he had never done so before but I knew he was severely stressed.

But instead tears welled up in his eyes and he slumped into a chair. The words of confusion he uttered have been lost to me; I tried to explain that I thought it was what was best for her even though I didn't truly believe it myself.

It took a while before he was calm enough to even consider making the two hour drive. I asked him to just talk to her and maybe she could make him understand.

Maybe she could make us both understand; would our love for each other carry us through this – I hoped so.

When he left that evening I wasn't sure I would ever see him again. Would he be able to concentrate enough to make it to his destination?

Would I get a phone call from the police informing me that one member of my family had just killed another? Him her or her him; I honestly couldn't be sure which it would be.

I worried about his two hour trip and was so glad to get that phone call when he got to the city. I could hear the hurt in his voice; he was calling from the kid's apartment.

I didn't hear screaming or crying in the background so I figured the initial encounter went well; as well as could be expected.

He doesn't remember much about what they talked about that night but he managed to get through it without making it worse. That is why Rachel is proud of her dad; at that moment she felt he would come around – eventually.

It wasn't suddenly made easy because we all knew; it was just the start of how we would find the way in which we each would cope.

I knew it would be hardest for John; for twenty years he had a son that he was very proud of. John was named for his grandfathers and as a matter of tradition. Sammy was named for his grandfather. The end of a tradition – this could cause any man to grieve.

At the same time that we were dealing with Sammy; John was also dealing with the health of his father. John's father was suffering from the long term effects of being a diabetic and had developed dementia.

He was having problems recalling the names of his own children; so there was no need to tell him about Sammy.

We knew telling him could lead to problems and was out of the question but we felt we had to tell John's mother. She is a very open minded lady and we knew she would never turn her back on her grandchild.

The time for the phone call came and we were nervous but pleasantly surprised when her only reply was, "Ok, we thought he was just gay."

Total and immediate acceptance by her and John's sister and for the moment they were the only people we told.

They were a practice run and it seemed to have gone well.

John had only started at his new job location a few months before and that alone can be a stressful time.

Most of his colleagues knew he had two boys; how could he now tell them he had a daughter. Much like my reaction; you start getting ideas about how to explain what has taken place.

Could he trust telling those he knew would understand and risk it reaching those who might not?

John has a strong personality and he can be hard headed when he knows he is right; he can't be pushed around and will stand up for what is right.

But when you're not sure what is happening is right; how do you defend it to others. Yet you feel you have to defend it because this is your child not some stranger you can ignore.

In a male dominated environment how do you stand listening to the discriminatory jokes you once did?

Will the attitude of his colleagues change towards him; would they be able to be themselves around him anymore?

Would they talk behind his back; would they just avoid him?

Were they looks of pity or silent jokes?

No matter how concerned you are about how this will affect you; eventually you will turn your attentions back to the one person who needs you now-your child.

John had many questions and concerns as we all did. I know he wondered how he missed the warning signs that this was coming.

He is a great father but how can you convince yourself of this when you have feelings of inadequacy as a father. Where did he fail Sammy?

He didn't fail Sammy and neither did I; it takes a hard look at us each and every day to believe that.

The conversations he had with Sammy in those early teenage years may have given us clues. Sammy was not impressed with the "jocks" at school; they treated the girls as joy toys.

We didn't think too much of this at the time because we taught of our boys to respect women. And Blaine wasn't impressed with the jock attitude either. Both boys said that they would never treat women with disrespect.

Sammy loved his super heroes and many of them were female and he admired their spunk. We weren't too concerned that he wanted to be like them; we were proud of him.

Sammy always felt more at ease around girls and adults; but boys tend to bully him and he liked a pretty girl.

John's feelings are never far from the surface but he always keeps them close to his chest when dealing with Sammy. To him a father is there for his kids; he knows his child, understands them, motivates them, and gives them all they need to succeed.

He teaches them self-respect; he is a role model, a champion, the rock up on which his children thrive.

John now had even more concerns as a father; will my child find love, will she wake up from surgery and think it was a mistake? Will she be discriminated against for the rest of her life?

Will he be able to be as close to this new person in his life as he was with his son?

How do you talk to this new person; could he be able to have an adult relationship with his new person as his daughter?

Would he be able to get past the fact that she has taken his son from him?

John was also feeling the loss of the grandchild Sammy will never be able to give him. Rachel loves children and wants to be a parent; will John ever be able to accept her adoptees as his grandchildren?

I know he will never make anyone feel unwanted or unloved; perhaps he will be able to find in a granddaughter what he fears he will not be able to find in a daughter.

When John mentioned Sammy's transformation to Pam, a friend of ours, he talked to her about how Sammy kept saying to him that he knew he was a woman even though she was physically a man.

He just did not know how to answer that. Pam finally said to him, "Well, how do you know you are a man?" to which John answered, "I just know." That helped John a lot it was a simple response from a great friend, not a professional's clinical advice, but it really was a turning point in John's understanding.

John was concerned that his colleagues would judge him and Sammy; but then he said, "People may say that this is God's way of judging Sammy to see if he can make the right decision. Perhaps it is the other way around and

God is really judging them to see how they respond to Sammy."

Chapter Four

Nature – the influences brought to bear on someone or something as a result of the silent forces in the universe either through contact before or after birth. (my personal definition didn't bother to look up Webster's definition as it is my definition which effects how I see things.)

Or as some others might say, "simply the way things are" or "it is what it is". Simply defined but that really doesn't help me come to terms with the events of this story, I guess I need a more scientific approach.

Nurture – the influences brought to bear on someone or something as a result of human contact, be it love or a sprinkle of water (again my own definition for the same reason).

Can nurture influence nature? Can nature influence nurture? Professionals seem to think so, sending criminals to jail is thought to change their bad behavior, seeing a physician can certainly change the outcome of diseases, seeing a councilor can change how you feel about not being loved as a child.

Then does it really matter the influences of either nature or nurture? Is it fair to blame the outcome of events on either? Perhaps the word "blame" should be stricken from the vocabulary of man, at least when it comes to parenting, if you do your best and things still go array whom do you "blame"?

Whether events are controlled by nature, nurture or the gods of the cosmos, we as a human race are condemned to suffer through the ups and downs of life.

We as a human race need to accept, adjust to, contribute willingly, seek out advice, fulfill our destiny, and above all remain calm.

Things are going to happen, rejoice and sing out praise for we are destined to repeat the mistakes of our parents, annoy our children, curse the role of being a parent, look lovingly at our children, and curse their existence.

But at the end of the day all will come out right if we remember to laugh at ourselves all the while embracing the ones we love.

Growing up I never considered the debate about nurture or nature. As a parent I was fully convinced that nature couldn't throw anything at me that couldn't be overcome with the right kind of nurture.

Love and guidance was the saving factor for any bad behavior. Correct the problem early and salvage the child. They would learn by the examples set by their father and I; we were good people.

We each had our faults but they were not the type that would cause harm; I mean who doesn't leave dirty dishes in the sink or break wind at the wrong time?

The boys weren't perfect either; they had their moments when I wish that the hospital had a return policy. They had their share of temper tantrums in the middle of the store for all to see, said bad words out loud; wonder where they got those from?

But we made the necessary corrections and all seemed fine.

What could nature have up her sleeve to compare with super parents like us?

Illness was no problem: we would lovingly take them to the doctor for immediate cures.

Bad behavior – well all kids act out- love and understanding, putting rules in place (we explained the reason for rules of course, mustn't be the do as I say type of parent) and maintaining order.

We would love a child with a serious illness as much as a healthy one. John and I spoke often of this when I was pregnant with Sammy.

We feared the worst but hoped for the best as any new parent would.

There are other issues to worry about of course; society and the views of others aren't easy to ignore but it doesn't mean we eagerly accept them.

When I was younger I had several friends who were gay – both sexes. My best friends was Mark and David, they lived in a very nice apartment with their cockapoo, Sandy.

David and I worked together and saw each other daily and we all hung out together on weekends. They would try to embarrass me kissing in public or talking about other gays, and trying to convince me some girl was a guy in drag.

But I was much to modern for that to get to me; I enjoyed their company mostly because I knew I could be myself and no one was going to force a "date" on me.

They were great fun to be with.

• •

When I met John things changed; he wasn't as open minded and felt uncomfortable around my gay friends so after we were married I lost contact with Mark and David.

The debate will continue for a while on whether homosexuality is a nature or nurture product and a debate for another day.

At the time I didn't think about it one way or the other. It wasn't a problem I was going to have to deal with.

Twins —now that was a problem I thought I would have to deal with. The scientist with the old idea that twins skip a generation never met my family.

When I was pregnant with Sammy the doctor was sure I would have twins until the ultrasound said differently.

On last count there were some seven pairs of twins in my family going back to my grandmother.

She had a pair of mixed twins, my uncle had twin boys, my aunt had mixed twins, my cousin had mixed twins, my brother had twin boys, my sister had twin boys and my nephew had twin girls.

The first set of twin girls that we can remember.

But sadly no, my problem would not be twins.

When I dreamed of having my own family, openness and honesty was going to be my parenting method. I was going to show my children that there was nothing that they couldn't talk to me about. They would be free spirits, with minds open to the possibilities that life would have to offer them. I would be sure that they were molded by nurture not nature.

Handbook, who needs a handbook, isn't love and tolerance all that's needed; didn't we survive inspite of our parents not because of them?

Nature or nurture, what a silly, misunderstood concept, what could mother nature do that love couldn't undo?

If we install our values and ideas into our children then how could they possibly do wrong? We all have our ideas on that topic and it too would be a subject for an entirely different book.

There are the basic values - be kind to others, be respectful, and mind your manners. Culture has an influence on our values as does our environment.

Things such as religion, politics and social views remain hot issues.

Than as reality sets in and we grow and mature ourselves, we begin to see things through someone else's eyes – our parents. We may not agree with their methods but we rely on the values they instilled in us. Even I can see those values now, whether intentionally or as I suspect, purely by accident.

Guess they weren't so far of the mark after all, but be damned if we are going to tell them that. We struggle in silent denial of our inadequacies as parents, jumping from challenge to challenge hoping the outcome leaves minimal damage.

However, even today I consider my situation different, whether I am right or wrong on that point really doesn't matter.

What matters is how that thinking affects the outcome of this story.

Growing up I saw the effect strict rules, old fashioned thinking, or worse, no thinking at all had on my siblings, the girls getting in trouble, the boys running wild, and the cycle repeating itself with their children. It wasn't that my parents supported that type of behavior, quite the opposite.

The problem with strict rules and no direction on what the right choices are can result in the wrong decisions being made. Instead of explaining why the rules existed and what the benefits of them where, it was simply "Do as I say, I know best".

Deny anything to a child and immediately they are going to think, "If the adults don't want us to have it, it must be good" And they are going to go in search of it; often making bad choices along the way.

By some miracle I managed to figure out that what my siblings were doing was not what was best for me. Not because I thought my parents knew what they were talking about, I had already written their parenting methods off as outdated and uncaring.

I just knew that I didn't want to be like them, and wondered why my parents didn't put more effort into correcting their bad behavior. I put it down to lack of love and caring.

If I had given it more thought at the time I would have discussed with myself "the nature or nurture debate".

Would it have made a difference? Hard to say at this point, but it probably wouldn't have hurt.

When you are growing up you don't really take into account the effects nature and nurture plays in your life. You just dream of what you want to do when you are an adult; you don't even give any real consideration to how you are going to get there.

I was a great fan of the Nancy Drew/Hardy Boys Series of books. They were full of adventure and mystery; so of course those were the stories that I first tried my hand at writing.

By age 12 I was more interested in far of adventure books that took place in exotic Egypt or Africa. My favorite subject in school was geography; so I set my stories in the lands of tigers and pyramids.

Elspeth Huxley was a favorite writer of mine; I loved her stories of African adventure and dreamed of living her life.

She made it sound so romantic, how wonderful to be even a small part of such a life.

I could see myself laying back in a canvas chair, sketch book in hand; taking in the life around me. My books would be self- illustrated; the beauty would come through my eyes to my waiting readers.

I kept them hidden from my family; I didn't think they would understand; neither of my parents would read and my sisters read romance novels.

As soon as I was old enough I was going to, as George Bailey in "It's a Wonderful Life" said, "I am going to beat the dirt from this dusty old town from my boots", or something like that.

Writing was going to be my way out, the big city my destination. And at age 16, I left home, with high hopes and far too much ignorance of the world. We all feel that we are going to take the world by the tail and show it who is boss.

How quickly reality sets in, needing to eat and have a dry place to rest your head puts plans on hold. But I kept writing, kept submitting to publishers, kept dreaming of my big break, and kept dreaming of that big family.

I was going to have it all, and not only was I going to have it all, I was going to be perfect at it. Isn't it funny how our mind plays tricks on us, leading us to believe delusion to be reality. Nothing was going to stand in my way; I was going to be an independent, free thinking woman of the world.

I had dreams of traveling the world as perhaps a freelance writer. Exploring the jungles of Africa, climbing the mountains of Peru, and skiing down the Andes were to be just a daily event in the life of this well-travelled adventurer.

I would do it all and still be able to maintain the perfect home life with the perfect husband and perfect children, the ideal existence.

When we aspire to become parents we don't think of the intrusions that children will make on our lives, we think only of the joy they will bring. As much as I wanted to be a writer, I wanted to be a mom just as much.

I was the aunt of a dozen nieces and nephews and at age 13 I lived with my sister to help her with her three kids. And I worked summers as a nanny to a couple who had two children.

I loved looking after them, cooking their meals, cleaning, and telling them stories. Perhaps it was because I was very young at the time but I felt like I was running my own home. I tried to look after them the way I wanted to look after my own.

I didn't just want to be their mother; I wanted to be their friend. Someone they would not be ashamed to come to and talk about their first love, their dreams and wanting my advice.

There would be no reason to give up on my dreams of adventure, I would take my children along with me and they would grow into the worldliest young adults.

I carefully laid out every detail to accomplish my dreams, right down to the type of man I would marry and the number of children we would have.

To smell the beauty that every baby gives off; a magic that a woman longs for in her life; someone small and fragile to hold; someone who would depend on you; trust you and come to depend on you for all their wants and needs.

My children would be intelligent, well-liked, popular with classmates, loved by teachers, and best of all they would be successful in their future lives.

We all think we are going to do better than how we felt our parents did with us. Every generation thinks they know better how to raise their children than their parents did.

After all we learned from their mistakes with us, I wasn't going to be so strict and intolerant, I was going to be open minded and understanding. I wasn't going to be so old fashioned, I would not limit my children's' imagination with unnecessary rules.

I made it to motherhood; and have some success as a writer. While I was writing mystery/adventure stories and my poetry a part of me wanted to write something that would leave a philosophical influence on the world. As I experienced life several things seemed to be a possible topic but nothing became of them and now I know why – this is the book I was meant to write.

CHAPER FIVE

I met John at a time when we both still knew what we wanted out of life. It was 1988 and I was tired of the bar scene, what girl doesn't get tired of it at some point?

I tried a dating service; they were new at that time, still a novelty. John wasn't the first man I had gone out with from the service. Few of them came anywhere near what I was looking for and I had no intention of renewing my membership when it came up.

Then a phone call came from a guy who didn't sound any different from the others. But I figured one more couldn't help and set up a time and place to meet.

We talked all night and made arrangements to meet the next night. John was working on the road at the time, leaving home on Sunday evening and returning late Fridays.

I waited anxiously for his return each week; we seemed to have a lot in common, we both loved history and left home to look for something better.

He was a businessman who seemed to have a plan for his future. He was intelligent, good looking and funny. His family was small; he was the youngest of three children.

His parents were wonderful; his best friend was even a nice guy. I figured I had it made, I found myself falling for him. John and I had grown up not far from each other. But we had to travel to the other side of the country to meet.

Most of my friends were dating or married, a few even had kids and they often tried to set me up on a date with someone they said was a great guy. They worked blue collar jobs, seemed happy to be unhappy in their jobs and relationships.

They seemed to accept it as a fact of life and I felt they were a little too happy to sit over coffee and complain. Mostly about their other half, I won't say better half as they might disagree.

I wondered why they were together if they weren't happy, and why they had kids if you didn't seem to want them.

I was choosey about whom I dated because I knew what character traits I wanted in my children, the same ones I wanted in a spouse. I managed to avoid dating the men thrown at me by my girlfriends (friends who are girls - for those of you not old enough to remember the original meaning) who wanted me to date the type of men they found attractive.

I guess they wanted me to be as miserable as they were with their beer drinking, blue collared, and over-dominating partners.

I enjoyed my independence far too much to let that happen and any man who caught my eye had better be comfortable with that independence as I wasn't going to give it up for any man. I was fearful that with enough time passing, I would change that opinion out of sheer loneliness.

I wanted to be the one calling the shots, couldn't a marriage really be of equal partnership. Why couldn't I still retain my own views on independence, child rearing and marriage?

I didn't think that would be a problem since my spouse would have the same ideas on parenting and marriage. And I was pretty sure he wouldn't want me to give up my independence.

He would love me because of that not inspite of it. He would let me be me; he would be a modern, intelligent and distinguished gentleman.

He would be a business man with ambitions to make the most of his professional and family life.

I am a woman of the 80s idea of what the perfect life is to be. In those days the hippy movement was out of date, we were the baby boomers who were going to make the world better by handling things in a professional manner.

Technology and innovation was the way of the future, and independent women were an asset not just noise makers.

I often told my friends that my marriage would consist of two apartments-mine and his- and we would only get together on weekends.

I quickly surrendered myself to him and he swept me off my feet.

A short courtship later, a very short courtship later, we were married.

A sudden surprise package was headed our way and we couldn't have been more delighted. Shocked but delighted! Wedding plans were moved up, baby items lovingly placed in drawers, a new home purchased and future plans dreamed about.

First came Sammy, a mere 53 weeks later Blaine blessed us with his appearance. We were set to do everything we could to make our children happy and I never thought I would have to say goodbye to either child.

Marilyn Phillips

All too often you hear the statement, "a parent should never outlive a child", or "a parent should never have to bury a child."

I don't think anyone would disagree with either one of these statements.

Unfortunately it does happen all too often but with the help of one's faith (whatever that maybe), family and friends parents are able to grieve for your loved one. With time the grieving process allows you to move on and replace the memory of your loss with the memories of your loved one.

I do not feel that I am able to grieve openly for the loss of my son, circumstances stand in the way of my being able to let go and moving on.

Each and every day I am reminded of that loss and that inability to grieve. Someone else is there now and my loved one is cloaked in a new form that I can't recognize and I am confused about. This new person is still my loved one, but she is not my Sammy, he is within my reach yet so far away.

What will become of my soul? I feel that I am lost forever in a fog of despair because I cannot say goodbye.

What would fill the hole left behind? I now have a new person in my life who wants to be as much a part of it as the one lost to me.

Where will I find solace from the daily pain? I will have to eventually allow this new person access to my heart but I don't have to close my heart to the one who has gone.

How do I hide the pain of not being able to speak the name of my loved one? This new person in my life bares hatred for my loved one because she feels he has taken something from her in the way of a happy childhood. She hates that she was denied the ability to be loved and cheered for in the way that he was.

How do I hide the need to remember all the special memories but do so without feeling guilty that in some way I am doing something wrong? I think of them as my memories and I have a right to them but at the same time I feel that by remembering him I am denying her the right to exist.

When I held my first child in my arms, it never occurred to me that these questions in a few short years would become a part of me.

"Closure" it is a word often used when one is faced with a crises. The ability to let go of the feelings associated with the trauma of something like the loss of a loved one. That is accomplished in this instance by a chance to say goodbye with family and friends.

When a child is killed suddenly in an accident or perhaps in wartime, the physical presence of a body is there for you to see and mourn. A child missing in action is perhaps a bit different, there is hope for a while but eventually hope turns to sadness and letting go gives you the ability to mourn the loss.

But imagine a child taken from you without warning, you can't mourn, there is no body, there is no hope that one day they will return. They have vanished never to be seen or heard from again.

I don't have the luxury of being able to mention his name, see his face again, saying I love you one more time, saying "goodbye my love".

This isn't a child taken by a stranger, like a missing child, this isn't a child taken by a parent. This is a child taken away by someone even closer.

How do I let go? Do I let go?

Everyone has suffered some type of loss in their life time; grandparents are usually the first a child deals with, for adults the loss of a parent; sometimes a parent suffers the loss of a child.

Even children have to suffer the loss of a favorite toy or pet; we might not think it is the same but to them it is.

We grieve, we remember, we laugh, we cry, we move on.

A part of them will always be a part of us; a special memory, a memento, a picture; all give us comfort.

We tell stories about our loved one, we speak their name out loud, place their picture lovingly on the mantel.

All those things which make the pain tolerable are taken from me. I feel that she said to me that I could no longer speak the name Sammy.

John and I loved to tell our friends about the accomplishments of our sons. And they were probably tired of hearing about the ribbons and medals that we so proudly displayed around our home.

When Sammy received a leadership award for his contribution to his youth program and shortly after received a medal for the same we couldn't wait to send out emails to everyone.

Now suddenly all those accomplishments belong to someone else who doesn't want to acknowledge them. They are just another reminder that he achieved these honors not her. That he was the one to get the hugs of pride and words of praise not her.

Now suddenly the pictures are gone, not destroyed; just taken from me and hidden away from me and even though I know where they are I am not allowed to retrieve them. I keep them hidden in boxes and drawers because I feel guilty about having them and loving the person who they are about. Suddenly all the mementos I ever possessed of my love one are removed from my house, they are no longer within my reach. They are locked up and I have the key but I am unable to retrieve them.

When John and I speak of the times with Sammy we are confused, do we speak of them as the memories of Sammy or Rachel.

We start by saying, "Do you remember when Sammy....", then we stop.

She doesn't want to hear that name and even when she is not around we feel guilty using his name and not hers when we speak of the past.

Sammy is a big part of our lives, how can we push him to the back of our minds? When I think of him I begin to cry because I don't want to lose him or his memories.

I will never again be able to talk with him; hug him, see HIS smile or see his children grow.

I can't have a picture of him in my pocket or on my mantel, only in my heart. I can't show to others all the accomplishments he had. I can't boast of him becoming a pilot, earning an award as outstanding youth for his contributions to his community.

I can't show off the pictures of him each time he was promoted in his beloved cadets – from private to Warrant Office Second Class- just one promotion from the top rank.

I can't tell all about the over 600 hours he put in as a volunteer at our local hospital or show the picture of his graduation from high school and how handsome he looked.

My dreams are filled with the visions of my beautiful Sammy. I see his face from a distance but the outcome is always the same. I see him across a field, on a corner, coming in the front door. But he turns away from me and when he turns back it is no longer him, instead she faces me. My heart aches as I feel the loss.

I can't talk to the people I meet and the people I have known for years about Sammy. I live in fear of how they will react; some will even shun me, laugh at me, and ridicule me.

The tears I want to shed for him can only be shed in private because no one is allowed to know my loved one is gone.

How can I handle it? I can't talk, I can't cry, I can't grieve, but I can carry on. The only question is – HOW.

No body to bury, no body to grieve over, nothing!

This is the struggle which greets me when I wake up in the morning, plagues me throughout the day and sometimes makes me cry myself to sleep at night.

All the parenting books in the world can't prepare you for this, you live and you learn and if possible you try to pass along what you have learned to others so that they may fair better then you.

The details are many but the message is this:

LIVE –LOVE-UNDERSTAND

AND BELIEVE IN THE POWER OF ONE – YOURSELF.

I assure myself that one day this new person will see the value in the one left behind; see the contributions he made. There will no longer be anger towards him just pride in what he did to help make the future possible.

Our new daughter will one day see the value of our Sammy as the person who gave her strength to become the person she is and help her succeed.

It is then that we will be able to once again show the pride in our Sammy that he deserves and we will celebrate him with this new person in our lives.

———————————————————

We all have our coping mechanisms and mine is to always be in control. If I feel like I am leading the way on something then I think I can fix anything.

This was one area in which I had no control; how was I going to cope this time? My Sammy was being taken from me; would I be able to have the same kind of relationship with this new person.

Would I be comfortable in public with her?

Would I be ashamed or appalled when I saw Sammy as Rachel for the first time?

How would I introduce him/her; to me they were neither?

"This is my son oh I mean daughter named......"

My family knew I had two boys now suddenly we have a boy and a girl; I wasn't sure how they would react. Will my family members understand when we tell them?

Even though John and I grew up close to each other; our families are very different. My family lives in a small fishing village and has had very little exposure to the outside world.

Whom do we tell?

Whose business is it anyway?

Maybe start with someone easy who you think will have a positive reaction.

I am afraid my first encounter with her didn't go as smooth as I had hoped.

Remember that drive back to my home when I was suddenly so informed of this transformation.

His father was away at the time and it was just Sammy (as Sammy) and myself; he was going back home by train and he asked if I felt comfortable if he traveled back home as Rachel.

He said he didn't like being Sammy anymore and he was supposed to stay in character as Rachel for his therapy.

I didn't scream in shock, I managed to control it but I am afraid I told him I wasn't comfortable enough with the idea yet.

But I promised to work on it for the next visit; he smiled and kissed my cheek.

Throughout this whole process I am grateful for the times when I didn't hold up my end in the support department so well; he was able to understand and flashed me that smile.

The feelings of resentment I have about the loss of Sammy is there always at least for now.

When it came time for her to change her name officially I asked her if she would keep her middle name and feminize it.

Notice I have just switched from him to her, from this point on that is who it is.

Her old name used to be; "Samuel Patrick" and my pet name for her was Patty, and I used to call her "Patty Duke", maybe I knew something without realizing it?

Now she is "Rachel Patricia" and she is still my "Patty Duke".

The next few years wasn't going to be easy; the things that you have to deal with are those that just come naturally in any other situation.

Like which bathroom do you use?

Do you tell potential employers?

Will you get hired if they know?

Can they legally not hire you?

Can they fire you?

These are questions which make it imperative that you know your rights because they won't be the same everywhere.

Where Rachel lives it is the law that she be protected from these issues. She couldn't be discriminated against because she is transgender.

That didn't make it any easier for her to get a job when she quit at the movie theatre. It took her over three years to get another job and during that time she still lived with her brother.

Her father was paying her bills; this only added to her stress and at times there was tension between us. But they all tried to stay positive and encouraged her to keep trying.

Soon the stress began to put a wedge between her and her brother and they decided they wanted their own apartments.

The price of a single apartment in their city was close to $1000 a month and there was no way either could afford that.

Blaine was working full time but making minimum wage at a fast food place, Rachel was still unemployed and her father couldn't pay for a place for her.

Their choices were small, move in with friends or come home to live; neither seemed a good option.

Blaine wanted to be in the movie industry and the city in which they lived didn't have a movie industry but the town in which his grandmother lived did.

Several months earlier John's father had passed away and his mother was alone; it didn't take her long to agree to let Blaine come live with her.

We found Rachel an apartment in the basement of a townhouse owned by a very nice couple; they took to her right away and kept an eye on her.

We hoped this breathing space would allow Rachel and Blaine to get back to a more civilized sibling relationship.

But it went better than expected and we both knew the road was going to be rocky both for her and for us. We were determined to make it through together as a family.

There was another person in this picture and it was important that he wasn't left out. Blaine wasn't happy and he let her know; and it caused tension between them.

Blaine was afraid that after all this work and going ahead with the surgery she would come to regret her decision.

He didn't agree with her decision and at the time there was nothing that would convince him otherwise. I have to give him credit he never abandoned her and began to call her Rachel.

He referred to her as his sister and when his friends asked he told him unwillingly and with obvious resentment. But when push came to shove John and I knew he would be there for her.

Slowly over the next few months we began to tell family and friends about Rachel. And much to our surprise all the reactions were the same.

Even my backward thinking family came into the twenty first century and accepted her all saying basically the same thing, that she knows what is best for her and as long as she is happy, why not?

"Why not?" indeed, I tried to tell myself nothing was different, I would adjust to seeing her as Rachel and I would slowly become comfortable around her.

The first time I saw Rachel I was surprised and very happy to see that there was a beautiful young lady wrapped up in that package.

One day we were out together and I happened to notice the looks she was getting from the young men; it was then that I knew she was into blossoming into a beautiful flower.

My Rose and her smile equaled anyone out there. She was happy. You could see it in her face, in the way she held herself and in the way it had all come together for her.

How could I or anyone deny this to her?

She was at last on her way to being truly happy.

CHAPTER SIX

Over the next year Rachel continued with her transition requirements, her hormones were making her breasts grow, she practices changing her voice to a more female sounding one.

I took her to a local cosmetic counter and had them show her the right cosmetics for her fair complexion. We did a girl's day out and went clothes shopping; I dyed her hair and we laughed together.

It was almost like old times!

Slowly the face of my beloved Sammy disappeared and was replaced by this new person. I knew she was my child, I gave birth to this individual, I watched over her for over twenty years.

I couldn't throw away those years and those memories but as I have said Rachel has a lot of resentment towards Sammy; she blames his existence on every bad moment in her life. If she had been born female all would have been right with the world at least in her mind.

She hated him and she told us so; how could anyone hate someone as good as Sammy?

She has tried to distance herself from him in every way. She neither wants to talk of the memories of the past or give credit to the person whose strength she has had to draw from to get to where she is today.

Yes, I love Rachel. She is my daughter and I am proud of the strength she has to face each day, what she has to face and still she keeps going.

I may find the strength to support her. Would I have had the strength to do as she had done to find her true self?

Probably not!

My wish for the future is someday she will be able to incorporate Sammy back into her life and once again he will be able to come back into our lives.

We aren't going to push her. It will have to be on her terms and in her own time. For now we will be the keepers of Sammy and all that he was; all that he is.

Perhaps Rachel felt she had to get rid of Sammy as quickly as possible or it wouldn't work. Perhaps that is why it was well over a year into her transition before she told me about what was going on and then I told her father.

At what point in her mind did she leave Sammy behind and become Rachel?

Looking back now it seemed it might have been as far back as age 16. As I remember back many of the signs were there.

She wanted to dress up as female characters when she went out for Halloween; I took it merely because she happened to like those characters and their shows.

She loved to wear wigs and high top boots; she had hidden several pairs of my shoes in her closet. She never turned down an opportunity to go clothes shopping with me.

She lived in silent pain for a long time and when she finally told me at age 18 how she felt depressed we still didn't catch on to the reasons why.

Counseling made her begin to look at herself as perhaps being transgender but when that idea was put to her father and I, John immediately rejected the idea and when counseling finished nothing was resolved.

Instead of keeping us in the loop Rachel decided to suffer in silence and went about each day pretending that nothing was wrong.

I started every day when she lived at home wondering if she was okay. I tried to get her to talk to me but instead she kept saying all was well.

In my heart I knew she was lying, there was no smiling anymore. I know now she was biding her time until she was on her own to do what she felt she couldn't do while living with us.

This is mostly where my anger comes from; why didn't she trust us to help? Not taking us into her confidence caused our Sammy to be abruptly taken from us.

We had no say in how he disappeared. We had no chance to say goodbye. If Rachel had allowed us the opportunity to adjust to the idea of her transitioning we would have been more helpful to her in those early days.

We felt like our legs had been cut out from under us. I would have loved to have been a part of helping her become the person she wanted to be.

As her mother I would have made the process easier. But she decided in her own mind that her father, brother and I wouldn't understand or approve. She was wrong.

We are all there for her now and we would have been there for her then. She subjected herself to unnecessary heartache by looking to her friends not her family for support.

Her friends instead slowly abandoned her while her family has stepped up to the plate and have become her support system.

She turned to faith for support and she found comfort in new friends she found there. But they knew her as Rachel and they had no idea of who she had been.

When they found out from someone who knew Rachel that she had been born a male; the church members quickly forgot about the wonderful female that they had come to know and made friends with.

Instead of being there for her and support her through what was going to be a trying time; they chose to turn their backs on her and tell her she was a sin in GOD's eyes and she was no longer welcome in the church.

She lost the one place where she felt safe and found comfort.

No, I am not saying we would not have had the same concerns from the very beginning; I do know we would not have abandoned her.

We would have had more time to prepare both ourselves and Rachel for the tough road ahead.

I just want to make it a point for those who think they may be transgender not to let fear get in the way of forming the right support system – family.

Talk to them early, let them know what is happening, let them help you, give them time to adjust, give yourself time to understand and reflect on what is best for you.

Rachel left things too long, it has caused her to be angry at not just Sammy and I am sure us, but at the world for failing her.

And now she feels the whole world owes her and she is filled with anger. And that anger has been there for too long.

Each and every day I worry about how she is doing; will her temper get her into serious trouble.

Things have to be just right, or as she perceives them to be right before she is happy and if things aren't orderly enough her Obsessive Compulsive Disorder kicks in.

She is not scared to tell her bosses so in no diplomatic manner. I fear she will be fired and that would upset her father greatly.

Not only do I have to deal with the way in which she reacts to things I have to deal with her father and the way in which he reacts to how she deals with things.

I often fear she may be suffering from depression or perhaps mood swings. When the phone rings I shudder to think how she may be feeling at that moment.

I want to bring her to live with me so I can look after her the way a mother should but I know it is not practical.

She will have to learn to make her own way in the world and I hope she can. There are days when I feel she will never reach her goals. There are days when I feel like I have failed her.

I know she doesn't think I have been as helpful as I should have been and she doesn't remember the good times we had together.

She was very happy about how her daddy accepted her transition; she knew her father had his own issues about the GLBT community.

I was a little slower and she understood that I had a closer relationship with Sammy; she was just surprised that I was a little slow in showing my support.

And she is right mostly because I only thought of my loss. My ideas of being the accepting, modern thinker were challenged.

It took time but I have managed to pull myself together and become the supportive parent I always hoped I would be.

I know she feels depressed about what she perceives to be the loss of her childhood. I just don't understand why.

She feels that all those accomplishments she made as Sammy deprived her of the opportunity to have that herself, as her true self.

She hates him for stealing her life from her, because he was loved not her, because he got the praise and he stood in her way.

She says she is proud of how we handled everything once we found out and I know she is grateful that she had us when the time came for her to have her surgery.

There was no way we were going to allow her to go through that alone.

Before being approved for surgery Rachel had to go through several psychological evaluations.

I always made sure that I was there with her for those so that the doctors knew that she had her family support.

Her father was unable to come with us because of work obligations but he wrote a letter which he hoped explained his support of Rachel.

We thought that the process would take a long time; it seemed so many were waiting for so long to be approved.

Within a few short weeks, she heard the news that she was fully approved. She was so excited; she emailed us and we could almost feel her excitement just by her words.

Rachel's surgery was scheduled for January and her father and I made arrangements to be there with her.

The procedure was to take place in a different city and John made arrangements to take time off from work. We both were unsure of how long she would be in hospital in case complications arose.

It was a private hospital and she was to arrive several days before the surgery and stay at their hospice before moving over to the hospital for the surgery.

She was to be in the hospital for several days and then return to the hospice for the remainder of her recovery days. It would be nearly three weeks in total.

After her recovery she would need to come home with us for another month to fully recover before returning to her own home.

She went by train to the hospice and a few days later her father and I followed; we stayed at a nearby hotel.

The evening we arrived we went and picked her up and took her for dinner. When we arrived we were surprised to see so many others there who were undergoing the same procedure.

We were horrified to see that only one other person had any family members with them. Rachel was happy to see us; she smiled proudly as she introduced us to everyone.

I was proud of John and myself at how well we presented ourselves. We weren't showing any signs of embarrassment; and believe me there are plenty of times when you can slip and say the wrong thing.

The nurses explained to us what was going to happen over the next few days and we listened proudly as they told us how beautiful a daughter we had.

Our fears of whether Rachel was doing the right thing, was slowly beginning to be removed from our minds.

I had never seen her so happy!

She was bouncing around like a little kid at Christmas.

When the day of the surgery came, we decided that instead of waiting around in the hospital we would walk around the mall close to our hotel.

We spoke little of the surgery instead trying to keep our minds busy with the fruitless mall walking.

When it was time for her to be coming out of surgery; we headed to the hospital. What would we find?

Would she be the new and happier Rachel; or would she have changed her mind at the last minute?

I know which one her father hoped for, secretly I hoped for the same.

When we arrived she was late getting out of surgery; John was getting more anxious as the minutes ticked off.

Then she appeared from around a corner and it seemed she was still smiling from the night before. She was still groggy from the meds but reached out for her father's hand.

After they settled her in her room we went in to see her; we sat by her bed for several hours before she was awake enough to talk to us.

When she awoke she was the happiest child in the world and I was glad to be able to be a part of it. Her daddy had bought her a fairy ornament from the mall and had placed it on her table; she always loved fairy ornaments.

After a short talk, she fell back to sleep this time with her daddy standing by her bed and her hand holding his under her chin.

When we had time to speak with her nurses in the hospital they couldn't stop talking about what a strong woman she was.

At first they thought we were Rachel's friends or support network. They were very surprised when we said we were her parents.

We asked them why, it was then that we found out that the majority of persons in transition have no one to support them. They come to the hospital alone and they leave alone.

We assured them at no time did we ever consider not being there for her. She was our daughter now and forever.

I made the remark that she was just the same stubborn know it all, just in a different package.

It brought smiles to everyone; the staff there knows it is a tough situation and a little humor never hurts.

When we were ready to leave to go home we were concerned about leaving her. Rachel loves her hugs and when we weren't there she would ask the nurses for some.

As we were leaving the nurses called out to us and said, "Don't worry we will give her lots of hugs."

We knew she was in safe hands!

We had to return home because John had to go back to work and I had to get Rachel's room ready for her to come and stay with us in our home.

She would need a lot of medical supplies as she had to have dressing changes several times a day and monitoring to make sure she didn't bleed excessively or get an infection.

What was to be my job?

And I took it on willingly; I wanted to show Rachel that I loved her and was behind her. I was excited to be able to once again have to look after my child; after the kids left home I suffered with empty nest syndrome.

She would not be able to walk about so I would have to tend to her every need. Including checking her wound to make sure it was healing properly.

I had no reservations about looking at the area; to me it was just like when she was a baby and I had to change her diaper.

The appearance of her change didn't shock me; in fact, I barely noticed the change. I can't explain it; it seemed perfectly natural to me as if I had been doing it all her life.

She was my baby that was all there was to it!

When it was time for her to come home from the hospital I went by train to bring her back. She wasn't able to walk very fast so we did a lot of joking about that.

When I was having problems walking a few years back she would hold my arm and help me along; now I was doing the same for her.

I joked that I could finally out walk her.

After a few weeks she was able to get up and about much easier; she even managed to make it to the television room for a little entertainment.

When she was chosen to have her surgery we were not sure when she would get an appointment date and her father and I had already made plans to go on vacation in mid- February.

We joked with her that she had better be up and about by then or she was on her own. We knew that she would be fine by then but still there was no way we were going to leave her alone.

Fortunately for everyone her friend Jane was going through the same transition and agreed to stay with her while we were away. Jane had also visited her when she was in the hospital.

By the time we returned from vacation she was ready to return to her own apartment. We drove her back that following weekend. She was still not able to return to work for another month but she was able to look after herself.

Her friend, Jane, lived in the same city and was very close at hand in case she was needed. Our good friends Edward and Maggie lived a few blocks from her; and were always there to help.

They were often a god send in times of crisis for both our kids. Many a day they were called into action when one of the kids needed something. They were there for them when John's father passed away and we were out east.

By mid-may Rachel was able to go to work at her fast food job. She is currently looking for a position in the animation jungle.

I say jungle because it seems like it to someone who is on the outside looking in. she did attend college for a year but didn't feel it was for her so she began to teach herself.

She was always good at drawing and now she is fantastic. The things she can draw in 3D blows my mind. I know her stubborn nature will not allow her to stop reaching for the stars when it comes to the things she wants in life.

She has already proven her strength!

And we are very proud!

CHAPTER SEVEN

Just what does it mean to be transgender?

When we are born we are identified by our sexual organs as being male or female – this is called gender identity.

Those who are transgender do not feel like they are a match with their physical or gender identity. They feel a mismatch has happened somewhere along the way.

Males identify more with females and females identify with males.

Because society puts labels and expectations on people transgender people will feel out of place in those roles.

For example: a boy may prefer to go shopping and wear his hair longer or feel a need to dress differently than what is expected of him.

A girl may prefer to be active in more male orientated sports, be more tomboyish and be very active. In this day of feminism, women's liberation and girl power few people see this as transgender or even odd.

They don't feel like they fit neatly into the societal package.

Society dictates that as a certain gender we act accordingly. The rules are unwritten but very much in our face on a daily basis.

Sammy never felt like he fitted in with the jocks at his school. He thought them brutish and didn't like the way they acted towards the female population.

He loved music and drawing; he had girlfriends from as early as age 10 and he always felt more comfortable in the company of adults.

He loved children and could never pass by one without cooing over them; his motherly instincts were present from an early age.

When do people feel "different" or "out of place in their own bodies"?

According to scientific research this differs with each person. Some know at a very early age that they should be identified as the opposite gender.

Others find it hard to identify the problem; they just know that something isn't right.

Like those who are gay; transgender people will suffer from confusion and emotional upheaval; especially as they go through puberty when their hormones are already in turmoil.

Some may think that they are gay; others may have no idea what is wrong and worse, have no idea where to go for help.

There are resources out there and I want to give you some ideas of where to go to get the help you need.

There are resources out there for you; read, read and read again. Talk to someone; a friend, a parent, a teacher or your doctor.

Don't try to go it alone!

A mental health professional knowledgeable with transgender issues will be the best resource for you. You're not crazy so don't be afraid to talk.

Those who know they are transgender will have decisions to make. And you will need all the information you can get your hands on.

Some like Rachel will make the decision to transform their bodies to the gender with which they identify. This is not an easy step as we will explain later but you may feel it is one that is right for you.

I am not making the decision for you by giving you the information; I am just advocating that you make the right choice for you.

It is a long and difficult process and not one from which you can turn back. It is one with which you will have to live each and every day.

Certain transgender people have made the decision that surgery is not for them; they are happy to live with their bodies as they are and prefer to merely live as the opposite sex and dress accordingly.

Some even takes names to identify their new found identity. Still others find it difficult to make a decision one way or the other, and make small changes like a name change.

There is often confusion about whether gender identity is just another name for sexual orientation. They are actually two completely different things but one person can have both.

Sexual orientation refers to one's emotional or physical attraction for another person

Just like a non-transgender person, a transgender person can be gay, lesbian or heterosexual.

One of the issues that face transgender people is the confusion about their sexual orientation.

For example: a male having feelings of belonging in a female body may feel they are also gay if they are attracted to a male because they have not fully understood the transgender issue.

In today's society you would hope that a better understanding if transgender issues would be widely known. Unfortunately this is not the case and it may be sometime before society catches up with the times.

Discrimination against transgender is still a huge issue and will remain so until people are educated about the causes of being transgender.

Like homosexuality, transgender is not a life choice. It is a medical condition thought to be caused by chemical changes in the brain while still in the womb. A mixed up message sent to the brain that identifies it as one sex while the body is sent the opposite message.

Scientist still continues to look for a reason while you struggle to get through the day. There is no reason for you to be alone.

As family and friends of a transgender person we will have our ups and downs. How does one approach someone who is identifying as transgender?

How can you relate to them? What do you say?

There are no easy questions and for the person struggling with being transgender there are no easy answers. As for you and your loved one, education is the best weapon.

Educate yourself about the meaning of transgender; seek out support groups, talk to professionals such as a mental health doctor and read as much as you can.

Don't try to go it alone emotionally; seek help from medical professionals. This will be an emotional roller coaster ride for you as well.

Find ways to talk to them which will be gender neutral, don't worry if you slip up occasionally I still do.

Be patient on days when they are moody and on days when you are moody let them know why. They will understand.

Above all don't stop talking with your loved one. If they don't feel like talking, simply say, "You may not, but I do".

Let them know that your feelings are important too. Just remember that road goes both ways, if they feel like talking and you don't, listen anyway.

As parents of a transgender child, familiarize yourself with local laws regarding the rights of transgender people. Not all levels of government will be the same.

Advocate for the rights of transgender people. You have a very high stake in this now and you have the right to speak out.

Discrimination against transgender persons is high and many are displaced because of it. Loss of jobs, relationships, housing, medical care, education and loved ones are a daily occurrence. Even the right to use a public restroom will be an issue.

Don't let your loved one become a victim.

Those of you who are not directly associated with a person who is transgender don't think that your responsibly is nil.

We as a society have the responsibility to stand up for any one person or group who is being unfairly treated.

We can all remember when homosexuals were the target group and although things are better for them it is still not perfect.

Many groups can relate to discrimination – natives, black persons, disabled persons, and the mentally ill.

We all have our biases, no one is perfect but together we can make a change. You can believe me when I say these issues are not going away.

Medical associations say that although it is impossible to have an accurate number, the cases of transgender are more prevalent in males then in females.

The law has not caught up with the times in the matter of transgender people. Many countries are however trying to make inroads into legal protection for transgender people.

In 1994, the term "Transsexual" in which Transgender falls, was replaced with the term "Gender Identity Disorder".

In 2011 a private members bill was put before Canada's House of Commons. The bill introduced an amendment to the Canadian Human Rights Act to include gender identity and to protect gender variant people from discrimination. The criminal code would identify offences against such persons to be the same as racially based crimes. The bill was passed by the Canadian Senate and is now the law.

In the U.S., a similar bill has been introduced and continues to be stalled by legislatures. While certain states and cities have taken the issue on, New York being the first to successfully pass legislation.

With the next generation being more sensitive to the issues of gender identity hopefully there will be an increase in tolerance as these issues gain more support.

Hopefully there will be a day when a person is judged not by their bodies but by their worth as a person.

Transgender issues have been around since recorded time and they were accepted members of society; often undergoing surgery to alter their genitalia.

If you have watched any documentary on ancient times you are well aware of the use and effects of castration. It was an accepted part of society and the ancients were also fully aware of the effects castration had on the male body.

I am not going to describe here how gender reassignment works that is something which should be discussed with you by your doctor. The risk of misinformation getting out there when surgical procedures being described by a non- professional is too great.

Needless to say there is a lot of information on the web and Sammy was directed by his doctors to a certain site which they felt was helpful. Your doctor will do the same; if they don't I would look for a new doctor.

Parents and loved ones don't be afraid to read up on this subject as well; if you are going to be there for your loved one (and I strongly suggest that you do) you will need all the information that you can get.

Having a loved one telling you that they are transgender isn't an easy thing to hear. No matter how modern a thinker you say you are. I would be lying to you if I said different and you would know it.

Still you're a person of the modern age. You have no prejudice against anyone; you live and let live.

If your child told you they were gay you wouldn't panic; you have heard and seen a lot of successful people who are homosexuals.

You still like them; never bothered you before why would it now? You would love your child no matter what.

You would be supportive, give advice, help them adjust, cautiously tell family and friends. You keep telling yourself, you're ok with this.

Besides your kids are not living at home anymore; you will only have to really deal with it on holidays. Come on that is what you were really thinking and your child knows it.

But they aren't going to hold it against you because they themselves are dealing with it as it happens. So you're safe!

I know of what I say because those were my very thoughts as well. I would handle anything; John and I got them through the trauma of those horrible school years.

May I remind you of those feelings that I said came that day of Sammy's announcement. They don't go away; they just get a little more manageable.

John and I fought hard against our first instinct to yell at him and ask what the hell he was thinking. Tell him there was no way we were going to allow him to throw his life away. No way in hell we were going to say it was ok to kill our beautiful son.

The son we loved, have wonderful memories of and whose love we didn't want to lose. How could we just stand there and say nothing?

But you have to hold your tongue, you have to listen and learn. You see the need on his face; you know in your heart that something was different with him.

All those years of being taunted and called names; if you look back can you see where things changed?

Should you have done more about those issues then? Was it your entire fault that you didn't get a handle on this earlier? Was there something lacking in your parenting skills that caused this?

Believe me when I say these questions and more are going to be going through your head. There aren't going to be any quick and easy answers.

But as the loved one of a transgender person you can't, shouldn't give up. We didn't and believe me there were many days when we wanted to. Would it be easier to walk away?

How do you walk away from your child? How can you stop being a parent? How do you slam the door and say no more?

Can you do these things? John and I couldn't; and today we are so glad we didn't.

There are days of ups and downs and I am hopeful that they will get better. We are still new to this and we are stumbling our way through but we are learning.

If I can just pass a few words of wisdom along to you that will help make this easier then I will be satisfied.

When Sammy made the decision to go through transition from male to female; he had to start a process that would take two years to complete.

His first task was to live as a female for two years. This would give him a sense of how he felt in a female body; he would dress in female clothes, and be called by his female name, "Rachel"

There were no hormone treatments until his doctor felt that he was a candidate for the transition and he was fully capable of handling the long process ahead.

He had to endure the looks of people, come out to his friends and come to terms with the realization that not all of them would be supportive.

He had been very active in the cadet movement and was friends with many of them. Would he be able to tell them?

He didn't have any problems doing any of those things. He seemed to know in his heart what he wanted and he was determined to have his way.

Sammy was always strong minded; stubborn some would say. And when he knew he was right he didn't let anything get in his way.

I remember one day he called me from school to bring his text book from his pilot bag (yes, he is a pilot). When I arrived at school he was waiting for me and grabbed the bag from the front seat of the car and called out that he would explain later.

When I arrived at the end of the day to pick him up he was ready to explain. Apparently his teacher had marked a question on his test as wrong and he was sure it was right.

It was a question about aerodynamics; well he showed the teacher and convinced her that he was right and he got his extra point.

So his father and I knew he could do this if he was sure it was what he wanted.

Steps

That didn't take away our concerns and there were many.

How was he to pay for any surgery he needed?

How did they make the decision about if he was a candidate?

What were the criteria by which they made their decisions?

Did they just do anyone who asked?

How safe was such a procedure?

Did it all happen at once or over several surgeries?

At what point could he change his mind?

What stats were available on the number of transgender persons?

What if he went through with the surgery and then felt he had made a mistake?

What would recovery be like?

What were the mental implications of someone dealing with being transgender?

Was it a mental or medical condition?

Would he just look like male wearing female clothing after surgery?

What would be the life- long effects in terms of his health?

What complications would we be expected to deal with?

The list of questions can be endless and frightening.

But with or without our support Sammy was going to do this. We made the choice that we would be there for him/her.

It wasn't about us; we knew it would have a huge impact on us in many ways but our life wasn't on the line; Sammy's was.

He had been depressed for some time and even told his father and I that he had thought of emasculating himself. He wanted the surgery and he wasn't being patient enough to get through all the steps needed.

He would call me in tears saying it was never going to happen. I assured him it would and we would be there for him.

His father was very upset and was taking it much harder than I was and he needed answers. Sammy made arrangements for his father to go with him to his next appointment with the psychologists.

John came away with a better sense of what was going to happen and I think a better understanding of Sammy's problems. But it didn't put him at ease; nothing was going to make losing his son of twenty years acceptable.

The road ahead was going to be hard on John and he knew it but he wasn't going to let his little guy down.

In closing I'll just say that if only one person finds hope from my words when I will say this book will have been worth the time I put into it.

If one person finds hope and strength from Rachel; I know she will think the book was worth it.

My entire family hopes that it will make the world more informed of an issue much misunderstood.

I hope in the future you will go into a situation with an open mind and when a person reaches out to you, you will extend a hand of kindness.

You will be pleased with the pleasure it gives you and you will be overcome with the kindness given back to you.

LIVE – LOVE- EXPLORE – FORGIVE

AND THE WORLD WILL GIVE BACK

TO YOU IN KIND.

Made in the USA
Monee, IL
09 November 2021

81653091R20090